SENEGAMBIA

THE KINGDOMS OF AFRICA

SENEGAMBIA

LAND OF THE LION

PHILIP KOSLOW

CHELSEA HOUSE PUBLISHERS • Philadelphia

Frontispiece: A view of Bulebane, the 19th-century capital of Bundu, a major state in the eastern part of Senegambia.

On the Cover: Soapstone sculpture from Sierra Leone.

CHELSEA HOUSE PUBLISHERS
Editorial Director Richard Rennert
Picture Editor Judy Hasday
Art Director Sara Davis
Production Manager Pamela Loos

THE KINGDOMS OF AFRICA
Senior Editor John Ziff

Staff for SENEGAMBIA
Editorial Assistant Kristine Brennan
Senior Designer Cambraia Magalhaes
Picture Research Patricia Burns
Cover Illustrator Bradford Brown

Copyright © 1997 by Chelsea House Publishers, a division of Main Line Book Co.
All rights reserved. Printed and bound in Mexico.

3 5 7 9 8 6 4 2

Library of Congress Cataloging-in-Publication Data

Koslow, Philip.
  Senegambia: land of the lion/Philip Koslow.
    p. cm.—(The Kingdoms of Africa)
Includes bibliographical references and index.

  ISBN   0-7910-3135-7 (hc)
  ISBN   0-7910-3136-5 (pb)

  1. Senegal—History—Juvenile literature. 2. Gambia—History—Juvenile literature. I. Title. II. Series.
DT549.22.K67 1996   96-32297
966.3—dc20   CIP

CONTENTS

Titles In
THE KINGDOMS OF AFRICA

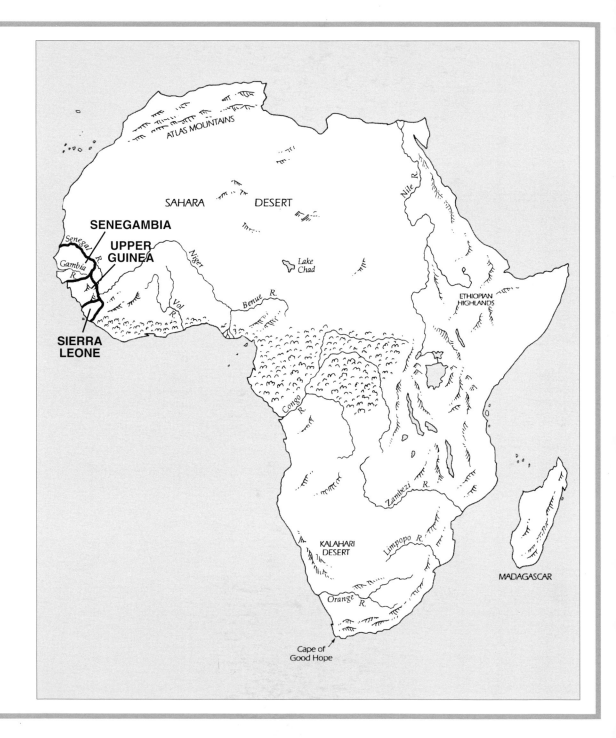

"CIVILIZATION AND MAGNIFICENCE"

On a sunny morning in July 1796, Mungo Park, a Scottish doctor turned explorer, achieved a major goal of his long and difficult trek through West Africa when he reached the banks of the mighty Niger River. Along the river was a cluster of four large towns, which together made up the city of Segu, the principal settlement of the Bambara people. The sight of Segu dazzled Park as much as the spectacle of the broad, shining waterway. "The view of this extensive city," he wrote, "the numerous canoes upon the river; the crowded population; and the cultivated state of the surrounding country, formed altogether a prospect of civilization and magnificence, which I little expected to find in the bosom of Africa."

Park's account of his journey, *Travels in the Interior Districts of Africa*, became a best-seller in England. But his positive reflections on Africa were soon brushed aside by the English and other Europeans, who were engaged in a profitable trade in slaves along the West African coast and who would eventually carve up the entire continent into colonies. Later explorers such as Richard Burton, who spoke of the "childishness" and "backwardness" of Africans, achieved more lasting fame than did Park, who drowned during a second expedition to Africa in 1806. Thus it is not surprising that, 100 years after Park's arrival at Segu, a professor at England's Oxford University could write with bland self-assurance that African history before the arrival of Europeans had been nothing more than "blank, uninteresting, brutal barbarism."

A physical map of Africa indicating the regions of Senegambia, Upper Guinea, and Sierra Leone.

7

8

This elaborately carved mask from Sierra Leone was one of the numerous great artworks created by Africans before their civilizations were disrupted by European colonial ambitions.

The professor's opinion was published when the British Empire was at its height, and it represented a point of view that was necessary to justify the exploitation of Africans. If, as the professor claimed, Africans had lived in a state of chaos throughout their history, then their European conquerors could believe that they were doing a noble deed by imposing their will and their way of life upon Africa.

The colonialist view of African history held sway into the 20th century. But as the century progressed, more enlightened scholars began to take a fresh look at Africa's past. As archaeologists (scientists who study the physical remains of past societies) explored the sites of former African cities, they found that Africans had attained a high level of civilization hundreds of years before the arrival of Europeans. In many respects, the kingdoms and cities of Africa had been equal to or more advanced than European societies during the same period.

As early as the 5th century B.C., when ancient Greece was enjoying its Golden Age, West African peoples had developed a highly sophisticated way of life and were producing magnificent works of art. By A.D. 750, ancient Ghana, known as the Land of Gold, emerged as West Africa's first centralized kingdom. When Ghana began to decline in the 12th century, power shifted to the empire of Mali, where the great ruler Mansa Musa became legendary for his wealth, generosity, and refinement. After the 15th century, Mali's preeminence passed to Songhay, which encompassed the great trading cities of Gao, Jenne, and Timbuktu; then to the dual kingdom of Kanem-Borno, whose ruling dynasty controlled the shores of Lake Chad for 1,000 years; and later to the remarkable fortress kingdoms of Hausaland, whose armored horsemen displayed their valor on the sunbaked plains. All these great nations were located in the heartland of West Africa, the vast savanna country known as the Sudan.

Much of the Sudan's wealth derived from the gold and ivory supplied by the peoples of the lush forest belt that extends along the southern coast of West Africa. Many of the forestland communities, which included Yorubaland, Benin, and Asante, had established themselves around the same time as the states of the Sudan had developed. But they were less known because the dense and forbidding woodlands shielded them from outsiders—until Europeans arrived by sea during the 15th century. At that point, the balance of power in West Africa shifted from the inland kingdoms to those on the coast; the forestland communities were drawn increasingly into the world economy, while the influence of the Sudan states diminished. The Sudan remained largely undisturbed by Europeans until the 19th century.

Not all of Africa can be divided neatly into savanna states and forest states, however. Along the West Atlantic coast, the regions known as Senegambia and Sierra Leone included elements of both forest and savanna. Furthermore, they enjoyed intense religious diversity, as traditional African religions vied for supremacy with Islam and Christianity. This stimulating and sometimes explosive mixture of cultures and terrains helped to initiate a unique chapter in Africa's rich history.

Chapter 1 | THE RIGHT OF FIRE

This low-lying section of Africa's West Atlantic coast is dominated by palms and mangroves; other parts of the region's remarkably diverse topography feature desert terrain, rugged highlands, lush forests, and rolling grasslands.

Senegambia occupies the West African coastal region where the vast Sahara Desert gives way to more habitable land. Subject to both parching heat and torrential rains, the region includes a wide variety of landscapes: the semiarid scrubland at the edge of the desert; the rolling grasslands of the savanna, whose expanse is dotted by graceful acacias and giant baobab trees; the mountainous plateau of the Fouta Djallon, the source of the region's great rivers—the Senegal, the Gambia, the Sine, and the Saloum; and the tangled mangrove swamps, receding into forests so dense that travelers can hear their voices echo off the foliage. Not surprisingly, the lands have been home to a vast array of spectacular wildlife. The rivers and streams teem with fish and with deadly crocodiles. Herons, egrets,

pelicans, flamingos, teals, and spoonbills gather at creeks and marshes. Herds of graceful antelope sweep across the open plains. Elephants cluster near the rivers, while lions, leopards, jackals, and hyenas roam the savanna.

In this challenging yet fertile region, black Africans have flourished for tens of thousands of years. At first they lived in small groups, gathering wild plants for food and following herds of animals, which they hunted for meat. Later, with the development of stone tools, Africans cleared forests and planted crops, which enabled them to live in larger, more settled communities. After 500 B.C., when iron tools came into use, settlements grew even larger.

Little is known about the earliest civilizations in Senegambia, but their successful adaptation to the land has been confirmed by the tools, pottery, and other artifacts discovered in the region by archaeologists. Among the most remarkable finds are the giant sculpted stones, known as megaliths, spreading over a large area near the mouth of the Senegal River. The stones vary in height from 3 to 12 feet, and because of their high iron content it is clear that carving them required a great deal of effort. One concentration contains 54 circles of stones, each circle measuring 18 feet in diameter. Near most of these circles are outlying stones positioned to the east, some carved so that they resemble the letter Y.

Scholars believe that the stone circles were burial grounds for rulers and priests, similar to Britain's Stonehenge. The outlying stones were most likely used to mark the movement of the sun across the sky. For example, when an observer stood in the center of the burial ground and saw the sun rise directly in the fork of a Y-shaped stone, he or she would have known that the winter solstice had occurred—in other words, that the sun had finished its yearly course across the sky and was now beginning a new cycle. This also may have had religious significance: according to West African traditions, life and death are part of a continuous cycle. It is likely that the markers of the sun's movements were located in burial grounds because the people of the time believed in a symbolic link between the cycles of the sun and the journey of the soul. In practical terms, observing the sun's course also helped ancient peoples decide on the best time to plant and harvest their crops.

By the 12th century A.D., the peoples who lived in the region between the Senegal and Gambia rivers had evolved into three main ethnic groups: the Wolof, the Serer, and the Fulani. Though each group spoke a different language, the languages were so similar—they are now part of the West Atlantic group—that Senegambians of different groups had little difficulty understanding one another. This was a great advantage, because it encouraged trade and the sharing of technology.

The essential tasks of the early Senegambians were clearing land and planting crops. Unlike Europeans, Africans had no concept of "owning" land. In their view, the land belonged to everyone and to no one. It had been brought into being by the creator god and remained in the care of the various

This 16th-century engraving shows West Africans practicing a variety of crafts. Long before the arrival of Europeans, the peoples of Senegambia had developed a self-sufficient way of life based on skills such as farming, weaving, and ironworking.

spirits who dwelled in the earth, the air, and the water. In Africa, an individual who cleared a plot of land had the right to occupy and farm it, provided that he honored the spirits and fulfilled certain requirements. The landholder was known in the Wolof language as *jom jen-gol* ("master by right of fire"). This title derives from the practice of clearing the land of trees and brush by setting fire to

14

A herdsman watering his cattle in the present-day nation of Senegal. Throughout the history of Senegambia, cattle herders have traded meat, milk, and hides for essential food items such as millet and rice.

a carefully marked off area and then using the ash from the fire as a fertilizer.

Each farmer worked a small plot of land no larger than five or six acres. The main crops of Senegambian farmers were sorghum, a grass similar to Indian corn, and millet. From the earliest times, farmers engaged in trade to supplement their diet. They exchanged their grains for fish caught by coastal peoples, and they obtained meat and milk from the Fulani herders who traversed Senegambia with their flocks of cattle, goats, and sheep, following seasonal variations in water supplies and pasturage.

Senegambia was rich in natural products that were extremely valuable to the local peoples. Its rocks contained iron ore that could be smelted and forged into tools and weapons. Along the coastline, valuable salt deposits formed when seawater evaporated in

A terra-cotta statue of a horse and rider from 14th-century Mali, one of West Africa's great empires. As early as the 12th century, mounted warriors from Mali began to invade Senegambia; as they intermarried with local peoples, they gradually established new patterns of social life.

15

lagoons and inlets. Inland, the soil nurtured cotton trees; pepper bushes; shea trees, whose fruit yielded a nutritious butter; and kola trees, whose nuts contain the stimulant caffeine and were made into a thirst-quenching beverage.

These commodities attracted traders from the Sudan, especially the Soninke from Ghana and the Malinke from Mali. Many of these traders, who spoke Mande languages (the dominant language group of West Africa), decided to settle in Senegambia, bringing with them new beliefs and new ways of life. The majority were Muslims—followers of Islam, the religion that had begun in the Middle East in the 7th century and had swept across North Africa and the Sudan. Traders were often accompanied by *marabouts*, Muslim holy men who tried to spread their faith by converting West African kings and chiefs to Islam.

Among the most influential newcomers to Senegambia were the Mande-speaking blacksmiths from Mali, who came because of the region's large supply of timber, which they needed to fuel their furnaces and forges. Because of their ability to transform chunks of rock into iron implements, smiths were often regarded as men who possessed magical powers derived from the spirits of nature.

They also had an affinity for snakes, which were regarded as sacred beings by most West African peoples. Not surprisingly, smiths were held in awe. But they were also feared and often had to live apart from the rest of the community. In his memoir, *The Dark Child*, Camara Laye, who grew up in Senegambia during the early 20th century, recalled his blacksmith father's strange relationship with a small and usually deadly black snake:

> As soon as I saw the little snake, I would run and sit in the workshop. I would watch him glide through the little hole in the wall. As if informed of his presence, my father at that very instant would turn his eyes to the hole and smile. The snake would go straight to him, opening his jaws. When he was within reach my father would stroke him and the snake would accept the caress with a quivering of his whole body. I never saw the little snake attempt to do the slightest harm to my father . . . . When my father felt that he had stroked the snake enough he left him alone. Then the snake coiled himself up under the edge of one of the sheepskins on which my father, facing his anvil, was seated.

While the traders of Mali adopted Islam to improve their relations with North African trading partners, smiths

(Continued on page 21)

16

WEST ATLANTIC MASTERWORKS

The artists of Africa's West Atlantic coast have been carving images in wood and stone for several centuries. Many of these artworks depict various spirits of nature and are used in religious ceremonies. Other sculptures represent the ancestors of prominent citizens; these have traditionally been displayed in family shrines, where succeeding generations can pay homage to their forebears.

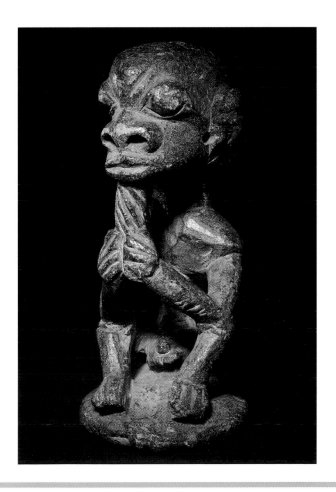

This sculpture by the Sherbro people of Sierra Leone was carved from soapstone. Works of this type, called nomoli, *were created before the 14th century, when the Sherbro were driven from the mainland of Sierra Leone by competing groups; they then settled on Sherbro Island, where they remain today.*

A bokorogi *mask created by the Toma people of Sierra Leone and Guinea. Bokorogi can be used only by members of the religious society known as* poro, *who employ the masks in their ritual dances. Each mask is believed to be the spiritual dwelling of an ancestor.*

This wooden sculpture, known as a byeri, was carved by an artist belonging to the Fang people of Guinea. (The figure's eyes are made of glass.) In the past, the Fang consulted byeri before embarking on important ventures, such as relocating a village or engaging in warfare.

A dugn'be *mask from the Bissago Islands, located off the coast of Guinea. During religious rites, dugn'be are usually worn by young men who have not yet been initiated into a religious society; the association with various dangerous animals indicates that the young men have not yet been "tamed" by the initiation process.*

(Continued from page 16)

continued to practice their traditional West African religion. They established themselves in Senegambia by forming religious groups, such as the secret *poro* societies, which took charge of relations with the spirits and thus wielded considerable power in the community.

But the power of the smiths was broken by a new wave of Mande-speaking migrants. These later arrivals were not craftspeople but mounted warriors, units of the fearsome cavalry that had founded the great empire of Mali. Between A.D. 1100 and 1500, waves of Mande warriors swept through Senegambia and conquered numerous settlements around the Gambia River.

Like most conquerors in African history, Mande warriors intermarried with the local peoples and adopted local languages and customs. In one aspect, however, these warriors changed the face of Senegambia forever. Before this time, Senegambians made no distinctions between social classes. Their communities were divided into clans, groups of people descended from a common ancestor, but all members of the clan were basically equal, even though the elders usually had the most authority. The Mande, on the other hand, had lived in larger kingdoms and had developed a form of social organization consisting of three distinct groups: so-called free men, including kings, officials, warriors, and farmers; hereditary groups of craftsmen, such as smiths, woodworkers, weavers, and fishermen; and slaves of various descriptions. This form of social organization, imposed by the Mande, led to the development of centralized kingdoms in Senegambia and introduced the region into the wider world of African politics. Among the local people who profited most from these changes were the Wolof.

21

Chapter 2 | THE SHAPE OF THE PAST

In this 19th-century engraving, a Wolof chief sits before his compound under the shade of a baobab tree. Beginning in the 14th century, the numerous Wolof chiefdoms of Senegambia were gradually organized into centralized kingdoms.

One of the favorite sayings of the Wolof is "Lammii ay ekkal demb" (Speech is what gives shape to the past). In accordance with this proverb, Wolof chroniclers recite numerous traditions concerning the birth of their kingdoms. One of the most popular stories takes place in the 14th century, when the Wolof still lived in scattered communities without kings or a central authority. One day, two villages bordering a creek near the Senegal River became embroiled in a heated dispute over a supply of wood. The villages were about to go to war when an aged man suddenly emerged from the creek, divided the wood evenly, and disappeared.

The villagers wanted to bring the old man back and make him their chief. They pretended to have another quarrel, and when the ancient figure emerged from the creek again, they seized him and held him prisoner. But the old man, whom the people called Father Sam-Sam, refused to eat anything and began wasting away. Finally, all the women of the village began to dance alluringly before Sam-Sam, hoping to restore his interest in life. To the delight of the villagers, Sam-Sam showed a special interest in a young woman who was smoking a pipe as she danced. Before long, he had taken two wives and begun a long, peaceful reign as the ruler of the region.

Sam-Sam's son, Mam-Pate, who succeeded his father, extended his power far beyond the original two villages until he held sway over the entire Wolof country. Assuming the title of *bur*, he created an empire made up of several provinces, each ruled by a chief: Walo, Kayor, Baol, Sine-Saloum, and

Jolof, the seat of empire. Mam-Pate was a wise ruler and left his own sons a stable and prosperous realm.

During the 16th century, however, one of Mam-Pate's descendants, Bur Gelem-Sambagene, began to abuse his position of power. One day, he summoned Amadi-Ngone, the chief of Kayor, to the royal palace. In order to demonstrate his superiority, the bur made Amadi-Ngone and his attendants wait outside the palace walls, without even sending them provisions. After eight days, Amadi-Ngone returned home in a rage. Realizing he had gone too far, Gelem-Sambagene sent a courier after Amadi-Ngone asking him to return, but it was too late. Amadi-Ngone raised an army and soundly defeated the bur's forces. From that point on, Kayor became an independent state, and the other Wolof provinces followed. Amadi-Ngone took the title of *damel*, by which the rulers of Kayor were known ever after.

The damels were traditionally crowned in Mboul, the capital of Kayor. Seated on a mound of sand, the new damel would hold a pot of millet seed while the high officials of the court placed a turban on his head. He then would be taken to a sacred wood, where he took part in traditional religious cere-monies. At the same time, a Muslim holy man guided the damel in various rituals of purification. (Like many West African monarchs, the damels adopted Islam to foster relations with Muslim traders, but they continued to honor the traditional religion to maintain the support of the people.) The damel never allowed his subjects to see him performing ordinary human activities, such as eating and sleeping. In this way he preserved the idea that he was a supernatural being. When the damel died, he was buried in a secret location.

Despite the mystical aura surrounding him, the damel did not wield unlimited power. On the contrary, Kayor possessed a complicated structure of government in which the damel shared power with a group of high officials. The women of the royal family, known as *linger*—the damel's mother, maternal aunts, and sisters—also possessed great power. All of the linger received tribute from villages under their control, and some of them achieved fame as warriors.

In addition to the linger, the king relied on seven leading officials (*kangam*), six of whom governed specific regions of the kingdom; the seventh, known as the *fara-kaba*, commanded the royal slaves. The kangam were military commanders as well as administrators, and they were famed for their courage in battle. Without the support of these men, the damel could not control the provinces. Skillful damels could get their way by promoting rivalries among the kangam, but those who faltered would soon find themselves deposed by the kangam in favor of a rival within the royal family.

In accordance with the exalted status of their residents, the palaces of the Wolof rulers were impressive structures. David Boilat, a 19th-century French priest of mixed African and European ancestry, wrote the following description of a typical royal residence:

> At the entrance there is a fairly large courtyard, at the door of which an armed sentry is posted. One passes through numerous other courtyards to arrive at the prince's quarters; between each courtyard there is a compartment used by bodyguards. The quarters of the monarch are always located at the rear of the enclosure. Next to them there is a large open court where he receives visitors, when the weather is good. To the right and the left one notices the quarters of his wives, the marabouts, and the palace servants, as well as storerooms, kitchens, and stables.

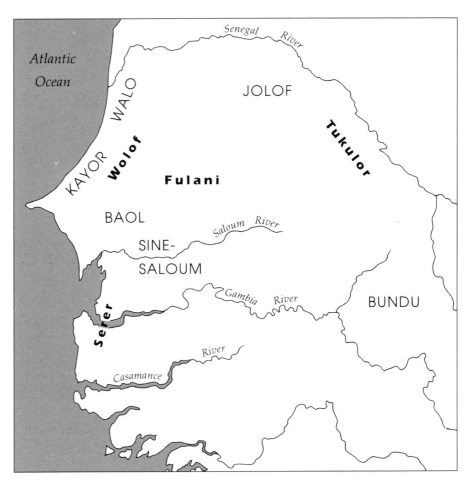

Despite the pomp of the royal court, the village continued to be the central unit of life in all the Wolof kingdoms. Each Wolof village comprised about 150 inhabitants. Their round houses with thatched roofs were clustered around a square, containing a well and a number of

A map of Senegambia, showing the major ethnic groups of the region and the five Wolof kingdoms of Kayor, Walo, Baol, Jolof, and Sine-Saloum.

25

Gora Mbengue's 20th-century painting of a hunter in extreme jeopardy illustrates the Wolof proverb, "If you knew what was on the lookout for you, you would drop what you are looking for."

them is known as couscous, which was slowly cooked over the fire in a large iron pot. While the women were engaged in the home, the men worked long hours in the fields.

According to their age-old traditions, the Wolof—and the other peoples of Senegambia—shared everything they had, not only with one another but also with strangers. As David Boilat discovered,

> White or black, known or unknown, anyone who travels among them can freely enter the first dwelling he comes to; the people will greet him, ask his name and the names of his relatives, and give him food and a place to sleep; they will entertain him during his meals and afterward. Finally, when he is ready to leave, they will say good-bye as though he were one of their best friends and will not accept any money.

The Wolof exhibited the same courtesy in all their day-to-day dealings. Upon greeting one another with the salutation "kene dou" (good day), they would inquire after one another's health and the health of family members by asking, "Mbar dhi-ame ngueuame?" (Do you have peace?), followed by "Mbar seu dhieukeur, diame?" (Does your husband have peace?), and so on. The reply to each question would be "Dhiame dale" (True peace). Finally, the

shade trees. The square was the public gathering place, and it included a platform on which the village elders sat and dispensed wisdom to the people. Most often, the eldest member of the largest clan served as village chief. His duty was to maintain order and to collect tribute payments for the king.

On a typical day, the women of a household would rise early to prepare millet for the day's meals. They pounded the grain in a deep wooden mortar, using a large pestle about five feet long. The millet was made into many dishes; one of questioner would exclaim, "Am dou lay!" (God be praised!).

When they were free from their daily labors, Wolof villagers loved to gather beneath the shade trees in the square and engage in conversation. Village gossip was far from their only subject: they also posed riddles and had philosophical discussions. Boilat, who had studied in France and was well versed in European culture, observed the following:

> [The Wolofs'] conversations revolve around useful topics; they always derive some benefit from them, such as we would derive from reading a good book, entering into a sort of dialogue with the author and deriving moral principles from it. If you imagine the Wolofs' meetings taking place in a room containing a rich library, where the president of the society would choose a book by a moralist and read it aloud to the gathering, each of whom would have the opportunity to express his reflections, you would have a true idea of their pastimes.

In their discussions, the Wolof would often refer to the sayings of various native philosophers. The most prominent of these was Cothi-Barma, who lived in Kayor during the reign of the great Amadi-Ngone and was credited with more than 5,000 maxims. Like the philosopher Socrates in ancient Greece, who was condemned to death because of his teachings, Cothi-Barma incurred the death penalty by protesting the damel's destruction of a village whose inhabitants had offended him. The philosopher tricked Amadi-Ngone into thinking he had been killed, after which he went on teaching in secret. On learning that Cothi-Barma was still alive, the damel had him brought to the palace. Amadi-Ngone demanded to know what Cothi-Barma meant by a new saying that was being quoted throughout the kingdom: "People do not gather under a barren tree." Cothi-Barma fearlessly replied that the barren tree represented a ruler whose pride and cruelty cost him the love of his people; a just king, on the other hand, could always count on the affection and support of his subjects. According to the traditional tale, Amadi-Ngone was so impressed by Cothi-Barma's wisdom that he resolved to become a generous and merciful monarch.

Unfortunately for the Wolof, not all of their kings heeded the sage advice of Cothi-Barma, nor did the many outsiders who played roles in the complex life of Senegambia.

Chapter 3 | SLAVERY DAYS

This 17th-century engraving depicts a group of Dutch traders showing their wares to West African clients. Trade relations between Senegambians and Europeans began in the 1440s and included a variety of goods, such as cattle hides, gum arabic, gold, ivory, and slaves.

Until the 15th century, the Senegambians' only contact with Europe had been through North African traders who brought small quantities of European goods. Because of the treacherous winds along the West African coast, European ships could not approach Senegambia by sea. But beginning in the 1440s, mariners in newly designed Portuguese ships reached Senegambia and made contact with the local peoples. One of these early explorers, an Italian named Alvise da Cadamosto, who had hired out his services to the king of Portugal, recorded the astonishment the newcomers felt as they saw the North African desert give way to savanna:

> It appears to me a very marvellous thing that beyond the [Senegal] river all men are very black, tall and big,

their bodies well formed; and the whole country green, full of trees, and very fertile; while on this side, men are brownish, small, lean, ill-nourished, and small in stature; the country sterile and arid.

The pale skin and long noses of the Europeans aroused an equal degree of wonderment in West Africans. But the people of Senegambia had been dealing with newcomers for centuries, and they quickly seized upon the new opportunities presented to them. Seafaring peoples such as the Kru hired themselves out to the Portuguese—and to the English, French, and Dutch who soon followed—piloting the European vessels along the coastline and acting as interpreters.

Although Europeans were welcomed as trading partners almost everywhere they visited, they were expected to adapt themselves to the customs of the country, following African trading practices and abiding by local laws when any disputes arose. They were allowed to live only in carefully designated areas, and their ability to travel was greatly restricted. (The restrictions were most severe in areas where African Muslims resided in large numbers, since Christians and Muslims had been battling in Spain and the Middle East for centuries.) Because many of the African states possessed powerful armies, there was little chance that Europeans would seek to violate these rules.

As the first foreign arrivals, the Portuguese were given special consideration by their African hosts. Those who were allowed to settle onshore were known as *lançados*. (This term derived from the expressive Portuguese phrase *lançados em terra*, "thrown on shore.") In addition to their trading privileges, the lançados were also permitted to marry African women; indeed, some chiefs bestowed their daughters on the foreigners, hoping to create profitable family alliances. By the 15th century, the children resulting from these marriages formed a thriving Afro-Portuguese community in Senegambia. Conversant with the customs and languages of Europe and Africa, the Afro-Portuguese were ideally suited to act as agents between European merchants and African leaders. Over the years, they were responsible for introducing into Senegambia a number of valuable new crops and commodities: pigs, poultry, and fruit trees from Portugal; manioc, peanuts, and papayas from the Americas; and bananas, coconuts, and mangoes from India.

For centuries West Africans had satisfied all their essential needs by trading with one another. However, many of the goods offered by Europeans appealed to them as luxury items that would enhance the status of kings, chiefs, and other prominent citizens: for example, glassware, jewelry, tobacco, liquor, cutlery, textiles, and weapons. In exchange, European merchants were eager to obtain many African products. Chief among them were malaguetta pepper, which grew abundantly in Senegambia; hides from cattle raised in the area; gum arabic, obtained from the bark of the African acacia tree and valued in the making of paper, candy, and textiles; and gold from the fields of Bambuk and Bure, which had generated the fabulous wealth of West Africa's great empires, ancient Ghana, Mali, and Songhay. In addition to all these goods, the Europeans traded for one more significant commodity: human beings.

Throughout most of West African history, slavery had existed in every society. When villages and kingdoms waged war against one another, the victors believed it was their right to take prisoners and dispose of them as they pleased. Often the captives would become the household slaves of chiefs and kings; in some cases, they would be sold to Muslim traders and transported to North Africa or the Middle East, where they were highly prized both as servants and as soldiers.

From the start of their relations with West Africa, the Portuguese were eager to obtain slaves. Some slaves were sent back to Portugal to work as servants. The great majority were put to work on sugar plantations that the Portuguese had established on islands off the coast of West Africa, notably São Tomé and Principe. Beginning in the 16th century, when the European powers were establishing colonies in North and South America, African slaves became the cornerstone of an expanding world

A 19th-century portrait of a Senegambian signare, an African woman married to a Portuguese merchant. Because signares usually inherited their husbands' property, many became influential figures in West Africa; their children often played a leading role in promoting trade between Africans and Europeans.

31

economy. Between 1500 and 1850, more than 12 million Africans were transported to the New World—the largest migration in human history.

The fate of the slaves transported across the Atlantic differed from the experiences of slaves within Africa. Although slaves occupied the bottom rung of the social ladder in Africa, they were nevertheless important members of the community. They were not considered property, but instead became part of their masters' households and often married into the family. Even if they married other slaves, their children were considered free. Slaves who served at the royal court or in the army often became powerful officials and military leaders. Many were in effect better off than the free men who had to earn their living by toiling in the fields.

Even the most degraded slaves remaining in Africa were better off than those sold to European slave merchants. Packed into the holds of slave ships—where many became sick and died—these unfortunates were transported thousands of miles to a strange land. There they were bought and sold like sacks of grain, despised not only for their low social standing but for the color of their skin. At the very beginning of the transatlantic slave trade, the Portuguese chronicler Gomes Eannes de Azurara recorded the plight of those about to be loaded into the ships:

What heart was so hard as not to be touched with compassion at the sight of them! Some with downcast heads and faces bathed in tears as they looked at each other; others moaning sorrowfully, and fixing their eyes on heaven, uttered plaintive cries as if appealing for help to the Father of Nature. Others struck their faces with their hands, and threw themselves flat upon the ground. . . . Their anguish was at its height when the moment of distribution came, when . . . children were separated from their parents, wives from their husbands, and brothers from brothers. . . . It was impossible to effect this separation without extreme pain.

The Slave Hunter, a 1985 painting by Gora Mbengue, depicts the capture of an unfortunate African. In Senegambia, slave hunters were often soldiers who engaged in slaving when not involved in military campaigns.

Beginning in 1700, Senegambia became an important slave-trading region, though in total number of slaves exported it ranked behind the Slave Coast of Dahomey, the Niger Delta, and Angola. Two and a half centuries later, Senegambia provided the backdrop for a vivid depiction of slavery's impact. Around 1964, the African-American writer Alex Haley decided to trace the history of his family back to Africa, something that no one had ever done. Haley had little to go on but a handful of family stories about an African-born ancestor named Toby, sometimes called Kintay, but his diligent research finally led him to Juffure, a village on the northern bank of the Gambia River. In Juffure, a local *griot* (historian) told Haley about Kunta Kinte, a Serer prince who long ago had been captured by slave traders. The griot's account meshed with everything Haley had heard from his relatives, and he realized that Kunta Kinte was his great-great-great-grandfather. The story of Kunta Kinte—who was taken from Senegambia to America, prevailed against the cruelties of slavery, and started a new family—became the basis of Haley's best-selling book *Roots*.

After their capture, Kunta Kinte and millions of his fellow Africans never saw

their beloved homeland again. Fortunately, though, permanent exile was not the fate of all enslaved Africans. Some of them—from Senegambia and other regions—who had the chance to return home eventually took part in one of the most dramatic episodes in West African history.

In this painting by Mor Gueye, European traders offer rifles to Senegambian slave merchants in return for captives. By 1700, Senegambia had emerged as one of Africa's largest slave-exporting regions.

Chapter 4 | LAND OF THE LION

A view of Freetown in 1798, six years after 1,200 liberated African slaves established the settlement on the coast of Sierra Leone. Despite many hardships, Freetown grew and prospered; by the 1860s, Freetown's population had increased to more than 18,000.

As ships make their way southward from Senegambia along Africa's West Atlantic seaboard, the monotonous chain of low-lying mangrove swamps is suddenly broken by a jutting, mountainous landmass. Impressed by the wild and rugged appearance of this land, one of the early Portuguese sea captains called it Serra Lyoa, or the Lion Mountains. With many variations, the name endured, and the area is now known as Sierra Leone.

By the time Europeans reached Sierra Leone, the region had been inhabited for thousands of years by a variety of peoples: the Bullom, Krim, and Vai along the coast; the Temne, Mende, and Lokko in the flat country; the Susu and Fulani in the mountains. Sierra Leone had no large kingdoms on the order of Kayor or Jolof in Senegambia. Instead, the peoples were organized into independent villages, each led by a chief. These chiefs enjoyed many of the privileges of West African kings. Among the Mende, for example, the chief was the only person allowed to wear jewelry made of leopard teeth, a symbol of supreme power, and he was carried about in a hammock by a group of courtiers who beat drums and sang his praises. The chief was also entitled to a portion of the crops and other goods produced by every family under his authority.

The Portuguese wasted little time in establishing relations with the inhabitants of Sierra Leone. As in Senegambia, they traded for various goods, including slaves, and before long Portuguese lançados had settled on the coast and along the major rivers. In some cases, the contact between cultures gave rise to exquisite works of art. Among the Bullom, for example, were craftsmen exceptionally skilled at the difficult work of carving ivory. The Portuguese commissioned the Bullom to make useful household items, such as spoons, sugar dishes, and saltcellars, to be sold to wealthy customers in Portugal. The Portuguese supplied the Bullom with European designs, such as floral patterns, and the Bullom executed these designs in a distinctively bold and expressive African style. The results were remarkable for their combination of sophisticated detail and emotional power.

Portugal's more powerful European rivals soon converged on Sierra Leone. By the early 17th century, Great Britain had established a strong presence in the area and had fought numerous sea battles with French warships ranging down the coast from their base at St. Louis on the Senegal River. Throughout these struggles, the slave trade flourished. By the late 18th century, approximately 75,000 slaves were being exported from Sierra Leone every year; nearly 40,000 of these were handled by British firms.

In 1772, in response to demands by British citizens, England's highest court freed all African slaves living in the country, and in 1807 the British Parliament outlawed the transatlantic slave trade. Though illegal slaving continued for decades, finally the tide had turned.

Most of the Africans living in Britain were domestic servants. Freedom would be a mixed blessing to them, since they had slender chances of earning a living in Europe. For this reason, a group of English antislavery activists—led by Granville Sharp, William Wilberforce, and Thomas Clarkson, among others—formed a plan to resettle liberated slaves in Africa. Sharp and his associates established the Sierra Leone Company, and after bargaining with a local Temne chief, they obtained 80 acres of land at the mouth of the Sierra Leone River as the site for the planned "Province of Freedom."

The first group of 377 settlers arrived in Sierra Leone in May 1787. These pioneers encountered enormous hardship almost immediately. The torrential summer rains began before they could build adequate housing; as a result, many colonists died of malaria

(Continued on page 41)

GLASS PAINTINGS OF SENEGAL

Senegalese artists have been creating distinctive glass paintings since the end of the 19th century, using a technique that came to Africa from the Middle East. The painters work on panes of glass that typically measure 13 by 19 inches; their subject matter includes historical scenes, glimpses of everyday life, and illustrations of proverbs.

The influence of Islam in present-day Senegambia is celebrated in this 1994 work by Babacar Lo. The painting depicts a Muslim leader, Sheik Ahmadu Bamba, in a place of exile where he is beset by evil spirits known as jinn. Resisting the influence of the jinn, Ahmadu Bamba prays and meditates while the angel Gabriel watches over him.

Hunted Down, *by Alexis Ngom, explores the peculiarities of human destiny. In the painting, a man has climbed a palm tree to escape a lion; he is unaware that a snake is gliding down the trunk and is about to bite his hand.*

Babacar Lo's Wedding Day depicts a Senegalese bride making the customary journey to the home of her husband's family. The women behind her carry her dishes and other possessions, while the procession is led by a Muslim holy man, or marabout.

In Jamu (1993), by Moussa Lo, a Wolof woman has her gums tattooed. In this process, the gums are pricked with thorns or needles, and lampblack is rubbed into the wounds. The dark coloration that results is highly desired by many Senegalese women, as it high-lights the brightness of their teeth.

(Continued from page 36)

and other diseases. A visitor to the colony wrote in her journal:

> It is quite customary of a morning to ask "how many died last night?" Death is viewed with the same indifference as if people were only taking a short journey, to return in a few days; those who are well, hourly expect to be laid up, and the sick look momently for the surly Tyrant [Death] to finish their afflictions, nay, seem not to care for life!

By 1791, only 48 of the original settlers remained, and the noble experiment of the Province of Freedom appeared to have failed. Around this time, however, a former slave named Thomas Peters assumed a decisive role in the colony's history. Peters had been living in Nova Scotia, Canada, home to a number of former slaves whose owners had sided with the British during the American Revolution (1775–81). When the colonists triumphed, pro-

This ivory cup is a splendid example of the art created by Bullom artists for Portuguese clients during the 16th century. Such items were a major element in the trade between Portugal and the various peoples of Sierra Leone.

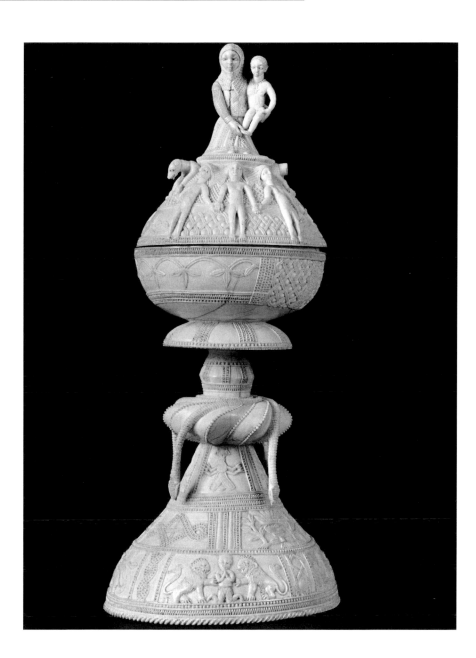

41

42

British Americans fled to Canada to escape the wrath of their countrymen, taking their slaves with them. Under British law, these slaves were freed, but they now lived in abject poverty. Peters arranged for their transport to Sierra Leone. In May 1792, about 1,200 Nova Scotians arrived in Sierra Leone and established a new settlement called Freetown.

Like the settlers before them, the residents of Freetown endured many hardships, including a devastating attack by French forces in 1794. They persevered, however, and their numbers increased steadily as British warships intercepted illegal slavers and brought their human cargo (known as recaptives) to Sierra Leone. The country came under the direct control of the British government in 1808, and some of the surrounding African peoples eventually migrated to the colony. By 1811, Freetown's population reached 2,117; by 1860, it had grown to 18,035.

As their numbers increased, Sierra Leoneans developed a distinctive blend of African and European cultures. In physical appearance, Freetown had a decidedly European atmosphere. The city was laid out in a grid pattern, with streets running at right angles to one

43

A view of Regent, one of the farming settlements outside Freetown. The success of the Sierra Leone experiment depended upon the ability of the settlers to grow crops on a large scale, a task to which they proved more than equal.

44

another. The typical house was built on a stone foundation, raised a few feet above the ground, and finished with timbered walls and shingled roofs. Looking out on the city from a hillside residence in 1841, a visitor wrote:

> Although there is sameness and formality in the long straight streets, crossing each other at equal distances, yet the irregularity of the different buildings, embowered as they all are in trees—the ships constantly in the harbor—the Bullom shore with its shining sandy beach and perpetual verdure—the broad blue sea stretching out till bounded by the horizon—form a relief to what otherwise might be considered tame and wanting in variety.

British organizations, such as the Christian Missionary Society, built a number of churches and schools in Freetown. Many settlers adopted Christianity, and several—among them Samuel Ajayi Crowther and James Africanus Horton—became prominent religious figures. Even as they adopted Christianity, however, many Africans also clung to their deeply rooted ancestral religions. African Christianity, like Islam before it, made allowances for traditional native beliefs within its doctrines.

Members of the Church Missionary Society, photographed in Sierra Leone in 1873. After the founding of the colony, numerous Africans converted to Christianity and attended British-run schools, including Fourah Bay College, the first university established in Africa.

45

46

The official language of Sierra Leone was English, a useful expedient considering the diversity of African languages spoken by the colonists: in addition to natives of Senegambia and Sierra Leone, the settlers included many peoples from eastern regions such as Aku, Yoruba, Igbo, and Hausa. The second generation of colonists—those born in Sierra Leone and known as Creoles—gradually developed a new language called Krio. Krio blended English with a number of African languages and even incorporated some Arabic words. Dr. Edward Blyden, a distinguished scholar of African history, noted the scope of the Krio language when he visited Freetown during the 1880s. Krio, he observed,

> has become something more than the only medium of communication known to the masses. It has acquired a sacredness of its own. There are certain ideas which have been expressed in it—certain images created—which lose their full flavor if rendered into other words. . . . It is the language of the domestic life, of courtship, of marriage, of death, of intensest joy and deepest grief. The people will not consent to speak of the private matters affecting their domestic well-being in any other tongue, any more than they would discuss such things in company with strangers. . . . It has sometimes a terse expressiveness which, in one single sentence, will convey an amount of satire or irony which would require a whole paragraph of English.

By the end of the 19th century, Sierra Leone had prospered from the growing trade in commodities such as palm oil and peanuts. A number of Creoles became enormously wealthy, occupying splendid houses in Freetown and enjoying a social life as opulent as that of any European merchant prince. For example, when the daughter of a prosperous Creole businessman named J. M. Thomas married C. C. Nicolls, a building contractor and city councillor, 1,000 spectators crowded into St. George's Cathedral, and 5,000 more lined the streets outside. The *Sierra Leone Times* covered the 1896 event, running a lengthy article that included an elaborate description of the jeweled and feathered gown worn by the bride in keeping with European tradition.

However they might resemble Europeans in their habits, the Creoles of Sierra Leone retained a pride in their African ancestry. As a British clergyman noted in 1874, Sierra Leoneans were determined to forge their own national identity:

> That education has made wonderful progress in Sierra Leone no one can doubt who has read the newspapers there, the letters and pamphlets of some of the leading native gentlemen of the Colony, and the sermons of some of the native pastors. . . . There is springing up a most natural and very proper feeling of independence and nationality. Whilst acknowledging the immense debt of gratitude due to Europeans, educated Africans are beginning to long to slip away from their European leading strings, and they are proving themselves perfectly capable of discharging all their duties as citizens . . . without foreign aid.

Independence from British control would not be won easily. The Sierra Leoneans would face many struggles before realizing this goal.

47

Chapter 5 | WAR AND DELIVERANCE

Though slavery may have ended fairly smoothly in Sierra Leone, in Senegambia the effects of abolishing the slave trade were ruinous. As in all of Africa's major slave-exporting regions, the trade had begun to dominate Senegambia's economy, corrupting every community it touched. In many cases, wars were fought for the sole purpose of taking prisoners to sell to slave traders. Besides depriving many regions of their healthiest, hardest-working individuals, these slave raids led to the rise of warrior groups, whose only motives were plunder and profit.

This was especially true in the Wolof kingdoms, which had always recruited their armies from the ranks of slaves. These troops, known as *tieddo*, were swashbuckling figures who sported long hair, earrings, and silver bracelets. Though phenomenally brave in battle, they had always posed problems in peacetime because of their excessive fondness for liquor, their distaste for honest work, and their habit of ransacking villages. As the slave trade grew, some of the tieddo began selling captives for their own benefit and became wealthy enough to establish themselves as local warlords.

Because they could not wage war effectively without seasoned troops, the Wolof kings were forced to tolerate the excesses of the tieddo: in Kayor, the saying arose that "the tieddo belong to the damel, and the damel belongs to the tieddo." However, the tieddo warlords made powerful enemies among West Africa's Muslims. Islam had spread

A group of tieddo, former slaves recruited into the armies of Wolof rulers. Having grown rich from plundering villages and trading in slaves, a number of tieddo became powerful warlords during the 19th century.

50

rapidly among Senegambian groups such as the Fulani and Tukulor, and these devout Muslims despised the tieddo for their lack of religious beliefs, their habitual drunkenness (Muslims disdained alcohol), and their practice of selling slaves, some of them Muslim, to the hated Christians. Conflict between Muslims and the tieddo in Senegambia had a long history, and Muslim marabouts often sheltered peasants threatened by marauding soldiers.

Throughout the 17th and 18th centuries, a number of Muslim leaders—most notably Nasir al-Din—had waged *jihad* (holy war) against Senegambia's kings and warlords. The Muslims had won some notable battles and had made numerous converts. But in the end, the kings had prevailed, and the Muslim warriors retreated to their strongholds in the Fouta Djallon region. By the early 19th century, however, Muslim power in West Africa became irresistible under such leaders as Usuman Dan Fodio and al-Hajj Umar Tal, who conquered the central Sudan and western Sudan, respectively. Their counterpart in Senegambia was Ma-Baa Diakhou.

Born in Kayor of Tukulor parentage, Ma-Baa embarked on his career of con-

quest after meeting with al-Hajj Umar Tal in 1850 and praying continuously for three days and three nights with the older man. Leading an army of about 5,000 men, Ma-Baa infused his campaigns with a distinctively religious aura. "On approaching a town he intends to destroy," a British official who observed Ma-Baa in action wrote,

> he dismounts from his horse, orders his praying carpet to be spread, and calls for writing materials. A staff of blind marabouts now surround him, repeating in a low chant that God is great, and that there is only one God and Mahomet is his prophet. Ma-Baa then earnestly writes grees or charms [believed to protect the wearer against wounds], which he hastily distributes to his warriors, who, as they now imagine themselves doubly armed, rush to victory or heaven.

Ma-Baa was ultimately victorious, but the ravages of his campaigns often created chaos. (When a British official warned him that his wars would ruin the country, he replied calmly, "God is our father, and he has brought this war. We are in his hands.") In previous times, the wounds of war had always healed, and life had gone on as before. But now, taking advantage of the disruption caused by the jihads and by centuries of slaving, heavily armed Europeans were delving ever deeper into the West African heartland.

The Europeans' encroachment on Senegambia came to a head in 1882, when Lat Dyor, damel of Kayor, resolved to prevent the French from building a railroad through the heart of his kingdom. For four years, the damel fought a tenacious guerrilla war against better-equipped French forces. When the French finally solidified their control over Kayor in 1886, Lat Dyor gathered his most loyal followers and took the field for one final battle, which occurred at Diakle on October 27. Though Lat Dyor inflicted heavy losses on the French, he and two of his sons lost their lives. (In keeping with Wolof tradition, Lat Dyor's followers hurried away with the damel's corpse and buried it in a secluded place whose exact location was never revealed.) Soon afterward

A Muslim holy man writing out a passage from the Koran, Islam's holy book, for a Senegambian client. Wrapped in leather or a piece of antelope horn and worn about the body, such writings were said to function as charms, protecting the wearer against harm.

52

the French occupied most of Senegambia, which then became part of the larger colony known as French West Africa. Britain, France's great rival in the region, managed to acquire only a narrow territory on both banks of the Gambia River (the present-day nation of Gambia).

Even in Sierra Leone, where relations between the colony and surrounding communities generally had been cordial, the disruption sweeping West Africa led to conflict. The trouble began when British officials tried to extend their control over surrounding areas. To finance their operations, they demanded that local residents pay a tax of five shillings for each house they owned. The Mende and Temne went to war, determined to drive the British into the sea. Sierra Leone's Creoles, having loyalties to both Africa and Britain, were caught in the middle of the conflict. One Creole who was briefly held by a Mende war party later reported a captor's eloquent condemnation of the actions of Europeans:

> The white men have come to our country and charge us whatever price they like for their goods, and give us whatever price they like for our produce. What they say we are willing to obey and have obeyed. Because we are so obedient you want to take our country from us by making us pay tax. We invited you to our country, and now you want to make us pay for the country which is ours.

A depiction of Muslim warriors in battle, by a modern Senegalese painter. Throughout the 19th century, Senegambia was disrupted by a series of holy wars led by Fulani Muslims who wished to establish Islamic regimes throughout West Africa.

53

As in Senegambia, the rapid-fire rifles and heavy artillery of the Europeans prevailed over the antiquated muskets of the African troops. After overcoming the Temne and Mende, the British extended their control well beyond the original boundaries of Sierra Leone. Whereas they had previously worked in partnership with the Creoles, the British now distrusted anyone with African blood. All Creoles were expelled from their posts in schools and government offices. These positions were filled by British officials, and the era of colonial domination began.

West Africa remained under European control throughout the first half of the 20th century. After the end of World War II in 1945, African demands for independence grew, and during 1960

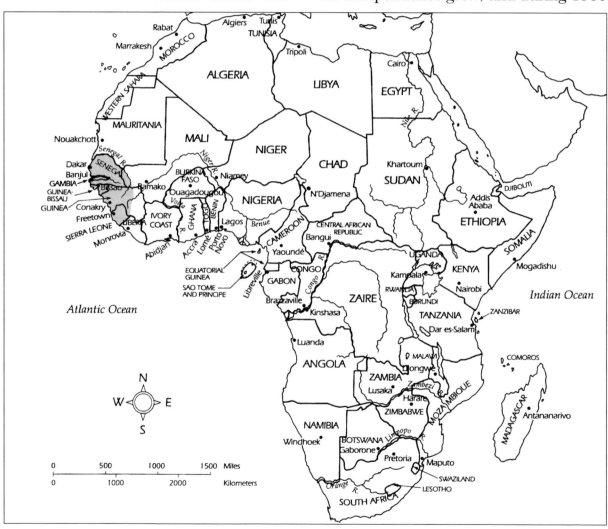

A map of contemporary Africa, with the shaded area indicating the regions of Senegambia, Upper Guinea, and Sierra Leone. From this territory emerged the independent nations of Senegal, Gambia, Guinea, Sierra Leone, and Guinea-Bissau.

54

and 1961, four new independent nations emerged from the colonial empires of the West Atlantic coast: Senegal, Gambia, Guinea, and Sierra Leone. (Guinea-Bissau, formerly Portuguese Guinea, won its struggle for freedom in 1974.)

In the years following independence, Senegal—incorporating the former Wolof and Serer domains—emerged as one of Africa's most progressive and stable nations under the leadership of President Léopold Senghor, who had been a distinguished poet and critic in France before leading the postwar independence movement. Under Senghor and his successors, Senegal has thrived as an agricultural nation.

Senegal's capital, Dakar, is a sparkling city of one million people. Its beaches and luxury hotels have made it West Africa's main tourist attraction. Farther inland, the entertainments and modern conveniences of the capital give way to rural areas where the people live much as their ancestors did, and welcome strangers with the same exquisite courtesy they extended centuries ago.

As this lively Dakar market scene suggests, the peoples of Senegambia have maintained much of their traditional way of life as they build a stable and prosperous modern nation.

55

CHRONOLOGY

c. 3000 B.C.   Permanent farming communities are established in the Senegambia region

c. A.D. 700–1100   Mande-speaking Soninke and Malinke traders migrate to Senegambia, mixing with established West Atlantic–speaking peoples

12th century   Wolof, Serer, and Fulani emerge as the major ethnic groups of Senegambia; Mande-speaking horse warriors begin to invade Senegambia, conquering villages and imposing new forms of social organization

Mid-14th century   Jolof becomes the dominant Wolof state under Mam-Pate

1440s   Portuguese ships make first landing in Senegambia; direct trade relations between West Africa and Europe begin

16th century   Kayor breaks away from Jolof control under leadership of Amadi-Ngone; other Wolof states follow suit

1650   Transatlantic slave trade begins to flourish; Senegambia becomes a major slave-exporting region as millions of Africans are transported to the New World

1772   Britain's highest court frees all African slaves in Britain

1787	Sierra Leone Company, formed by British antislavery activists, establishes colony in Sierra Leone with 377 liberated slaves
1792	1,200 Africans arrive in Sierra Leone from Nova Scotia, Canada, establishing a new settlement named Freetown
1811	Population of Freetown exceeds 18,000
1815	All European powers outlaw transatlantic slave trade; palm oil and peanuts replace slaves as main export from Africa's West Atlantic coast
1850s	Ma-Baa Diakhou begins series of holy wars in Senegambia, seeking to spread Islam and abolish last vestiges of slave trade; French steadily gain ground in the region
1882	Lat Dyor, damel of Kayor, begins war against the French
1886	Lat Dyor is killed in battle against French at Diakle; French complete their occupation of Senegambia, which becomes part of French West Africa
1892	Hut Tax War begins in Sierra Leone, as Mende and Temne protest British control and taxation
1896	Sierra Leone becomes part of the British Empire
1960–61	Senegal, Gambia, Guinea, and Sierra Leone gain independence

FURTHER READING

Boilat, David. *Esquisses Sénégalaises.* [Senegalese Sketches]. Reprint of the 1853 edition. Paris: Editions Karthala, 1985.

Brooks, George E. *Landlords and Strangers: Ecology, Society, and Trade in West Africa, 1000–1630.* Boulder, CO: Westview, 1993.

Curtin, Philip D. *Economic Change in Precolonial Africa: Senegambia in the Era of the Slave Trade.* Madison: University of Wisconsin Press, 1975.

Curtin, Philip D., ed. *Africa Remembered: Narratives by West Africans from the Era of the Slave Trade.* Madison: University of Wisconsin Press, 1967.

Davidson, Basil. *Africa in History.* Rev. ed. New York: Collier, 1991.

_____. *The African Slave Trade.* Revised ed. Boston: Little, Brown, 1980.

Davidson, Basil, with F. K. Buah and the Advice of J. F. A. Ajayi. *A History of West Africa, 1000–1800.* New revised ed. London: Longmans, 1977.

Forde, Darryll, and P. M. Kaberry, eds. *West African Kingdoms in the Nineteenth Century.* Oxford: Oxford University Press, 1967.

Fyfe, Christopher. *History of Sierra Leone.* Oxford: Oxford University Press, 1962.

Fyfe, Christopher, ed. *Sierra Leone Inheritance.* London: Oxford University Press, 1964.

58

Gamble, P. D. *The Wolof of Senegambia.* London: International African Institute, 1967.

Haley, Alex. *Roots.* New York: Doubleday, 1974.

Hull, Richard W. *African Cities and Towns Before the European Conquest.* New York: Norton, 1976.

Laye, Camara. *The Dark Child.* Translated by James Kirkup and Ernest Jones. New York: Noonday, 1994.

McEvedy, Colin. *The Penguin Atlas of African History.* New York: Penguin, 1980.

Park, Mungo. *Travels in the Interior Districts of Africa.* Reprint of the 1799 edition. New York: Arno Press / New York Times, 1971.

Rodney, Walter. *History of the Upper Guinea Coast, 1545–1800.* London: Oxford University Press, 1970.

UNESCO General History of Africa. 8 vols. Berkeley: University of California Press, 1980–93.

Webster, J. B., and A. A. Boahen, with M. Tidy. *The Revolutionary Years: West Africa Since 1800.* New ed. London: Longman, 1980.

Wright, Donald R. *Oral Traditions from the Gambia.* *Volume I: Mandinka Griots.* Athens: Ohio University Center for International Studies, 1979.

_____. *Oral Traditions from the Gambia.* *Volume II: Family Elders.* Athens: Ohio University Center for International Studies, 1980.

GLOSSARY

chronicler   person who writes or recites a detailed, continuous historical account of events

clan   group of people who claim descent from a common ancestor

courtier   attendant in a royal palace

couscous   food made by hulling millet seeds and boiling them until soft

damel   royal title given to the ruler of Kayor

lançados   early Portuguese travelers to West Africa, who were permitted to settle in African kingdoms and to intermarry with the native people

linger   collective term for the mother, maternal aunts, and sisters of damel in the African state of Kayor, which flourished around the 16th century

malaria   disease of the red blood cells, transmitted to humans through mosquito bites in tropical climates

mangrove   tropical tree or shrub that thrives along coastal areas

maxims   sayings of a proverbial nature, which usually urge sensibility and fairness

megaliths   very large stones used as monuments or in construction

pestle   a device for pounding grain into meal

savanna   terrain featuring rolling grasslands and open woodlands

semiarid   characterized by light rainfall and little annual precipitation

smelt   to melt minerals down in order to chemically refine them into usable metals

sorghum   tropical grass whose seeds yield a thick, sweet syrup; used to make porridge and bread

thatched roof   roof using layers of plant material, such as straw or leaves, as a protective covering

West Atlantic   African language group that includes Senegambian languages such as Wolof, Serer, Fulbe, and Tukulon

INDEX

63

PHILIP KOSLOW earned his B.A. and M.A. degree from New York University and went on to teach and conduct research at Oxford University, where his interest in medieval European and African history was awakened. The editor of numerous volumes for young adults, he is also the author of *El Cid* in the Chelsea House HISPANICS OF ACHIEVEMENT series and *Centuries of Greatness: The West African Kingdoms, 750–1900* in Chelsea House's MILESTONES IN BLACK AMERICAN HISTORY series.

PICTURE CREDITS